Moving Mountains

Jane Williams has taught theology at Trinity College, Bristol, and is currently lecturing at St Paul's Theological Centre, Holy Trinity Brompton, and Visiting Lecturer at King's College London. A regular contributor to the *Church Times*, she is married to Rowan Williams, the Archbishop of Canterbury.

Church Times Study Guides

Deliver Us: Exploring the Problem of Evil
Mike Higton

Doing What Comes Naturally? The Christian Tradition and Sexual Ethics
Neil Messer

Embracing the Day: Exploring Daily Prayer
Stephen Burns

Faith Under Fire: Exploring 1 Peter and Revelation
John Holdsworth

The Fellowship of the Three: Exploring the Trinity
Jane Williams

Here is the News!
John Holdsworth

Immersed in Grace: Exploring the Baptism
Stephen Burns

Living the Thanksgiving: Exploring the Eucharist
Stephen Burns

The Mighty Tortoise: Exploring the Church
Jane Williams

Prophets and Loss: Exploring the Old Testament
John Holdsworth

The Same But Different: The Synoptic Gospels
John Holdsworth

Who Do You Say that I Am? Exploring Our Images of Jesus
Jane Williams

Yours Sincerely: Exploring the Letters of the New Testament
John Holdsworth

Church Times Study Guide

Moving Mountains

Jane Williams

CANTERBURY PRESS
Norwich

© Jane Williams 2007

First published in 2007 by the Canterbury Press Norwich
(a publishing imprint of Hymns Ancient & Modern Limited,
a registered charity)
13–17 Long Lane, London EC1A 9PN

www.scm-canterburypress.co.uk

British Library Cataloguing in Publication data

A catalogue record for this book is available
from the British Library

ISBN 978-1-85311-787-9
5-pack ISBN 978-1-85311-788-6

Typeset by Regent Typesetting, London
Printed and bound by Gallpen Colour Print, Norwich

Contents

Leaders' Notes

Planning sessions

Remember

Keep in mind the ethos: 'The course is an attempt to share, not to talk down.'

There is enough material and exercises to offer a choice if you are having a single session: familiarize yourself with all material and select.

Prioritize

Choose the most important aims for your group. Deciding which aims to focus on will help you select the most appropriate material and exercises.

Decide the balance, in your local context, between learning aims relating to the course content and other needs (e.g. enabling people to meet socially, encouraging people to speak about faith). This will also help in selecting appropriate material and process.

Planning

Have a variety of different ways of working – e.g. discussion in twos or threes, discussion all together in plenary, one person talking, personal reflection, opportunities to write down, etc. Changing the pace aids concentration. Also people have different learning styles, and sessions are likely to work best if they include elements that cater to the variety of ways in which people learn.

Plan how the group will work through your chosen exercises. There are many ways of using the material.

When introducing new concepts or material, think whether there is any additional background information that might help people without much prior knowledge.

Decide what prayer/worship opportunities to include. Some may find it practical to have optional worship beforehand: others might want something that contrasts with the 'wordiness' of discussion.

Let participants know if they need to bring anything with them, or if you want them to do anything before the session.

Getting started

Sitting comfortably

A circle rather than rows encourages discussion/participation. Arrange seating so all can see each other's faces.

Forming the group

Make sure everybody knows who everyone is, and introduce the purpose of the session. Explain how it will be shaped and the time when it will end (make sure you finish then!). Using a quick introductory exercise can give each person an opportunity to give his or her name and say something. Give limits for contributions (e.g. 'one sentence'); otherwise they tend to get longer going round the circle.

Ground-rules/Boundaries/Group covenants

It helps if all are clear and agreed on how the group will run at the beginning. You may want to suggest a few 'ground rules' (e.g. not interrupting/confidentiality) and give the group a chance to suggest others.

Group facilitation

The leader/facilitator needs to attend to the dynamics and smooth working of the group, as well as the course material. Maintaining the group needs skills of encouragement and 'gate-keeping' to help people get involved and keep communication channels open.

Affirm contributions. If someone is criticized (by you or anyone else – and however well you know they can take it) it can discourage others, who may avoid comments or questions that might be risky.

Remind the whole group about the agreed ground-rules if and when necessary.

Concerns about those who participate too much or too little can often be helped by changing the process and giving people a task in smaller groups. The shy get an opportunity to speak and the over-vociferous can't dominate the whole group.

When you subdivide during a session, always have at least three sub-groups in a room. If there are two groups they listen to each other and get distracted.

Ensure people know they can raise questions and how to do it appropriately. Question time can operate in different ways, e.g.:

(a) Have a 'questions board' where people can put up questions (possibly written on 'post-it' notes) as they occur to them. Have time planned to address these.

(b) Gather in small discussion groups to raise questions – some people feel more confident voicing queries in a small group. Others in the group may respond to some, and the group can select a key question to contribute to a plenary.

Introduction

The word 'faith' is often used nowadays, but seldom examined. On the whole, the general use of it is slightly pejorative. 'Faith schools' are seen as selective, elitist and inclined to brainwash their pupils. 'Faith communities' are rather troublesome entities, which have to be consulted but which contribute little to life. People of faith are assumed to have made a life-style choice, which they are perfectly entitled to do, but not to foist onto others. Just as some people choose to be vegetarians, or marathon runners, so people of faith choose to believe in God.

At best, our society sees faith as a harmless eccentricity. It can be equated with believing in UFOs or horoscopes. At worst, faith is seen as dangerous fanaticism, which blinds its adherents to their duty to the rest of society. Either way, it is irrational and deluded.

This study guide will argue that the Christian faith simply cannot be seen as one way of life among a number of possible options. What Christians claim about God is either true or it isn't. If it is, it is about what the world is really for.

Precisely because it is faith, there remains an unproven element, and Christians who attempt to deny that seem to be trying to force God's hand and make him do things differently. For the time being, living in the world as though God is true involves trust and hope. But not stupid trust and irrational hope. It is based on experience and tested in the world. It is based on observation of the world and tested in experience. For some, faith starts in personal encounter with a God who reaches out to them. For others, faith starts in a set of questions about how the universe comes to be the way it is.

The start of St John's Gospel binds these two things together inextricably. It is because of the nature of the God who makes the world that we are able to encounter him. 'In the beginning was the Word, and the Word was with God, and the Word was God ... All things came into being through him', St John says. And so, 'He came to his own.' It is because the world is made by God, and because God is like *this* that faith is possible. God does not simply set the world in motion and leave it to its own devices. Instead, he communicates with it, from the start, encourages his creatures to be fully involved, and then comes and lives in it with us.

Faith in this God, then, involves living in such a way as to demonstrate what we believe about ourselves, our maker and our world. It involves commitment to certain kinds of action, certain ways of living, and rejection of others. It assumes that faith has both an objective and a subjective element, both an active and a passive. It assumes that there is a God in whom to have faith, and who will be there, whether we believe in him or not. He is not like Tinkerbell in pantomimes of Peter Pan, whose life can be extinguished by lack of belief from others. But it also assumes that if you do believe in God this belief cannot be held in such a way as to leave the rest of life unaffected. Faith changes how you live. It is in that sense both something given *and* something done.

That challenge and responsibility, with all its terror and its hope, is part of what this study guide sets out to explore.

1

The Assurance of Things Hoped For, the Conviction of Things Not Seen

To be sure of things that we are only hoping for and convinced about things we can't see does sound perilously like Lewis Carroll's Queen, who is proud of believing 'six impossible things before breakfast'. For many people, that is precisely what faith is – a determination to hang on to belief in God, despite all evidence to the contrary.

But the author of Hebrews only comes to this definition of faith in chapter 11, although faith is one of the main themes of the letter. Hebrews tells the story of God's consistent calling to his people and of their faithful response. But it also says that we who live after Jesus are in a new era of faith, one which our ancestors would have envied. So the majestic opening of the letter to the Hebrews says, 'Long ago God spoke to our ancestors in many and various ways by the prophets, but in these last days he has spoken to us by a Son.' The writer seems to be saying that now, instead of the messages from God which were all that previous generations had to go on, we have seen and heard from God the Son himself.

In other words, the author of Hebrews does not think that 'faith' is a wilful belief in something for which there is no proof. On the contrary, he thinks that there is quite a bit of proof, but still a large element of the unknown, the 'unseen'. A big part of what Hebrews sees as proof is the lives of other people. So, at last, in chapter 11, the writer looks at the people of faith who have gone before us, each of whom acted in faith and received some of faith's benefits, but died without having seen the whole of what they were waiting for.

Exercise

Read Hebrews 11.

- Identify what each of the people mentioned did in faith.
- Identify what each received for their faith.
- What might the author mean in verses 39–40?

What Hebrews sees is a pattern made from the lives of many, many people, and it predisposes us who follow them to believe in a God who shaped their lives and choices and might shape ours. Their faith, Hebrews says in 11.3, is that the world is made by God and has a purpose. That purpose is not always visible in everyday events, but its contours begin to show through the lives of people of faith. Through them, we begin to see that people are made to be in relation to God, and that the world is designed to find its completion in God. So the great climax of the argument of Hebrews 11 actually comes in the glorious purple passage in 12.18–24. The goal of lives of faith is to come to the 'city of the living God', with all those who, with us, before us and after us, have walked in faith.

This is what all the ancestors in chapter 11 have been waiting for – not their own individual fulfilment, but the consummation of all creation, living with God. For Hebrews, 'faith' is a vision about a whole and healed world, because if God is really what the faithful believe him to be, then anything less would be too small. So it is not an anticlimax that the vision in chapter 12 of humanity living with God leads straight into mundane instructions about day-to-day life in chapter 13: that is just as it should be, according to Hebrews. Those who live after the coming of God the Son know more clearly what they are destined for, and can begin to try to build a life together that can start to reflect what is hoped for, though not yet seen.

The community to which Hebrews was originally written did not have any clearer reasons for faith than any others. Reading between the lines (cf. 3.12, 12.7), some in this community are tempted to give up, or to see persecution and hardship as a sign that their faith was misplaced. That is why the letter is written with such urgency and passion – the author is trying to show the readers that faith is not irrational, even under such circumstances as theirs. Faith has shaped history and will continue to do so until it reaches its fulfilment.

Summary and definition

- Faith is believing that God has made the world for a purpose, which is to live with him.
- Faith is not irrational, but depends on seeing how faithful lives have shaped the world and have helped to make our own response easier.
- Faith is corporate. Because it is based on a vision of the God who creates and fulfils all that is, it draws us into life in a community that begins to imitate that vision.
- Past faithful lives and the faithful life of the communities we live in give us a basis for continuing to believe in God, even when things are not going well.
- It is usual to assume that the opposite of faith is doubt, but if the above definition is true, then it would be more truthful to say that the opposite of faith is accidie. Doubt is inevitable, until we see God's fulfilment. But accidie – the weary, indifferent, uncaring idleness that makes us give up on things, stop trying, stop aiming for any kind of goal – can destroy faith because it destroys the pattern of a faithful life. The people Hebrews talks about went on living lives of trust in God, even when they doubted, and so they were able to be part of the pattern of God's action that made faith possible for others. Lives of indifferent selfishness make it harder for others to believe that the world has a goal and that God will bring it to fulfilment.

Accidie – a pessimistic weariness that believes nothing can be changed or achieved.

2

'Faith is Caught, Not Taught'

Most people who have a religious faith could point to the people who gave it to them and who keep it alive. They may have caught it from friends, from families, from inspiring teachers or from a whole community, or a combination of all of the above, but faith in God, like faith in anything else, is nearly always contagious.

But of course this personal contact is only effective if what is offered makes sense. People do not, on the whole, 'catch' either religion or other commitments if they do not fit into any rational pattern of life, or help to make life more rather than less comprehensible. We will look later on at some of the most common reasons for denying that faith makes sense of life, but here are three 'testimonies' from great Christians who 'caught' faith, and who did so because there were issues in their lives of which Christian faith helped to make sense.

St Augustine of Hippo (354–430)

Augustine lived at a time when most people believed in God, or gods, or a divine realm of some description. His mother, Monica, was a Christian, but his father, Patricius, was not, until towards the end of his life. Augustine seems to have been fascinated by theology all his life, but it took him a long time to come to a faith that felt genuinely right and that made sense of the central issues in his life.

We know a surprising amount about Augustine because he wrote a very unusual book about himself. It is called *Confessions*, and it is actually an account of his search for God. Very few people of that period wrote such personal and honest accounts of themselves, and it was a particularly startling book for an influential church leader to write. This is not supposed to be edifying hagiography, but a genuine description of the struggles of one man to find God.

> **Hagiography** – telling the story of someone's life so as to emphasize their sanctity and leave out anything that might detract from that.

Augustine comes off the page very vividly. He was a clever, slightly wild boy. He knew that he was the apple of his mother's eye, and he found that both natural and exasperating. He made deep and lasting friendships that mattered to him passionately. He attracted helpful patrons and was all set for a starry academic career. But despite all these reasons for confidence, all these inducements to believe that life was just as it should be, Augustine was aware of a great restlessness and uncertainty in himself.

A lot of this seems to have centred on sin. This was partly a personal question for Augustine. He felt that he had lived a life full of varying degrees of selfishness and sin, from stealing apples as a boy for the sheer love of the adventure, to living for years with a woman to whom he was not married, and with whom he had a son. But although this sense of guilt undoubtedly added an edge to Augustine's religious search, his personal experience was backed up by observation and by theorizing. He noticed that no one is free from sin. He watched the way that tiny babies at the breast can still feel envy and anger, so that he was not convinced that sinfulness grows, but rather that it is a state into which we are all born.

> **Dualism** – the belief that the state of the world derives from a battle between good and evil, and that most material things, including human bodiliness, are a result of a partial victory of evil.

To begin with, Augustine found some coherence in a dualistic sect called the Manichees. They believed that the material world, including human bodies, are not the work of the true God. The divine realm is invaded by lesser, corrupting forces, and the divine element in human beings, the spirit, becomes trapped in gross flesh, awaiting release. The great advantage of this was that it allowed Augustine to believe that sin is not our fault and does not affect our essential being. What happens to our bodies is almost irrelevant, since all of that belongs to a lower order.

> **Manichees** – a dualistic sect that Augustine belonged to for a time. They attributed sin to the work of a malevolent power, but believed that the vital divine spark trapped in gross human flesh was untouched by sin.

But Augustine became increasingly dissatisfied with this account of creation. For one thing, he could not believe that all physicality is negligible. He writes of being ravished by the beauty of nature and of being drawn closer to its maker as a result. For another thing, the good god of the Manichees seemed intensely *passive*, as did the divine spark in human beings. The Manichaean god and his followers seemed to be able to do little about themselves or their world apart from ignoring it and hoping it would go away. Nor could Augustine finally convince himself that this account of sin made sense of his own feeling of being both helpless and yet responsible for our own sinfulness.

This was the heart of Augustine's intellectual and spiritual struggle, and his journey to faith involved both rational and personal conviction. His mother's faithful, implacable witness had an effect that Augustine was only able to acknowledge with affection later in life. He was also helped by the great and learned Bishop Ambrose of Milan, who satisfied the intellectual snob in Augustine, and made him realize that he did not have to give up his mind in order to become a Christian. Another vital link in the chain was a biography of St Antony of Egypt, who had given up all his possessions to go and live a life of extreme asceticism in the desert. Augustine felt personally challenged that someone so much less educated than himself had been able to respond so wholeheartedly to the call of God, while he was still dithering about.

Confessions describes Augustine's long, circuitous path to faith in Jesus Christ, which culminated in a garden, appropriately enough.

Exercise

Read Augustine's description of the moment of his conversion.

- What is his mental and emotional state immediately beforehand?
- What role does his knowledge of the life of St Antony play?
- Why do you think he hears children's voices?
- After this experience, Augustine lived a celibate life. His conversion involved a personal and permanent resolution of a problem that he called 'lust'. He then went on, for the rest of his long and influential life, working on the intellectual question of sin, as well as many other important personal and doctrinal issues. Partly, no doubt, as a result of his own experience, his theology emphasizes the free grace of God, which comes out to meet us and set us free from the chains that prevent us from acting as we long to.
- For Augustine, 'faith' involved a desire and an ability to lead a changed life. Before he could reach faith, he needed to be convinced both intellectually and in practice – he needed to see the difference.

The streams of my eyes gushed out an acceptable sacrifice to thee. And, not indeed in these words, but to this effect, I cried to thee: 'And thou, O Lord, how long? How long, O Lord? Wilt thou be angry for ever? Oh, remember not against us our former iniquities.' For I felt that I was still enthralled by them. I sent up these sorrowful cries: 'How long, how long? Tomorrow and tomorrow? Why not now? Why not this very hour make an end to my uncleanness?'

I was saying these things and weeping in the most bitter contrition of my heart, when suddenly I heard the voice of a boy or a girl – I know not which – coming from the neighbouring house, chanting over and over again, 'Pick it up, read it; pick it up, read it.' Immediately I ceased weeping and began most earnestly to think whether it was usual for children in some kind of game to sing such a song, but I could not remember ever having heard the like. So, damming the torrent of my tears, I got to my feet, for I could not but think that this was a divine command to open the Bible and read the first passage I should light upon. For I had heard how Anthony, accidentally coming into church while the gospel was being read, received the admonition as if what was read had been addressed to him: 'Go and sell what you have and give it to the poor, and you shall have treasure in heaven; and come and follow me.' By such an oracle he was forthwith converted to thee.

So I quickly returned to the bench where Alypius was sitting, for there I had put own the apostle's book when I had left there. I snatched it up, opened it, and in silence read the paragraph on which my eyes first fell: 'Not in rioting and drunkenness, not in chambering and wantonness, not in strife and envying, but put on the Lord Jesus Christ, and make no provision for the flesh to fulfill the lusts thereof.' I wanted to read no further, nor did I need to. For instantly, as the sentence ended, there was infused in my heart something like the light of full certainty and all the gloom of doubt vanished away.

(Augustine, *Confessions*, translation from www.CCEL)

Teresa of Avila (1515–82)

Teresa of Avila lived through one of the most turbulent periods of the Church's history. Although Spain was a staunchly Catholic country, it was deeply affected by the Reformation, in ways that directly impacted on Teresa's own life and theology.

Teresa writes about her own life mostly because the religious authorities of the Inquisition were quite suspicious of her, and she needed to reassure them that she was a loyal subject of the Catholic Church. Her monastic foundations and reforms had made her a high-profile figure in Spain, and she could not afford to get on the wrong side of the Church.

We have two main sources of information from Teresa herself about her life of faith. The first is her *Life*, and the second is *The Way of Perfection*. Neither is straightforward autobiography, because they are dominated by pastoral and theological concerns, not by a desire to lay bare

Teresa's own soul. But the woman we meet is ardent, attractive, unconventional and energetic. She tells us that she ran away from home at the age of seven, hoping to reach the 'land of the Moors' and gain martyrdom. Luckily – for her and for us – she didn't make it.

But although this episode suggests that religion was imaginatively important to Teresa from an early age, it was not until a teenage flirtation had almost, but not quite, reached scandalous proportions that her real vocation began to grow. She was sent away to a convent until the scandal blew over, but by the time it did, she was a novice.

It is not as clear with Teresa as it is with Augustine that there was a defining 'problem' on which her religious search is centred. But there is a clue in the account that follows.

Exercise

Read the following account from Book 9 of Teresa's Life.

- It is talking about a time when Teresa is already gaining quite a reputation for holiness and for being able to give instruction in prayer, and yet she clearly feels like a fraud.
- The turning point seems to be when she realizes that, in his loneliness and suffering, Christ might need even her:

My soul was now grown weary; and the miserable habits it had contracted would not suffer it to rest, though it was desirous of doing so. It came to pass one day, when I went into the oratory, that I saw a picture which they had put by there, and which had been procured for a certain feast observed in the house. It was a representation of Christ most grievously wounded; and so devotional, that the very sight of it, when I saw it, moved me – so well did it show forth that which He suffered for us. So keenly did I feel the evil return I had made for those wounds, that I thought my heart was breaking. I threw myself on the ground beside it, my tears flowing plenteously, and implored Him to strengthen me once for all, so that I might never offend Him any more.

I had a very great devotion to the glorious Magdalene, and very frequently used to think of her conversion – especially when I went to Communion. As I knew for certain that our Lord was then within me, I used to place myself at His feet, thinking that my tears would not be despised. I did not know what I was saying; only He did great things for me, in that He was pleased I should shed those tears, seeing that I so soon forgot that impression. I used to recommend myself to that glorious Saint, that she might obtain my pardon.

But this last time, before that picture of which I am speaking, I seem to have made greater progress; for I was now very distrustful of myself, placing all my confidence in God. It seems to me that I said to Him then that I would not rise up till He granted my petition. I do certainly believe that this was of great service to me, because I have grown better ever since.

This was my method of prayer: as I could not make reflections with my understanding, I contrived to picture Christ as within me; and I used to find myself the better for thinking of those mysteries of His life during which He was most lonely. It seemed to me that the being alone and afflicted, like a person in trouble, must needs permit me to come near unto Him.

I did many simple things of this kind; and in particular I used to find myself most at home in the prayer in the Garden, whither I went in His company. I thought of the bloody sweat, and of the affliction He endured there; I wished, if it had been possible, to wipe away that painful sweat from His face; but I remember that I never dared to form such a resolution – my sins stood before me so grievously. I used to remain with Him there as long as my thoughts allowed me, and I had many thoughts to torment me. For many years, nearly every night before I fell asleep, when I recommended myself to God, that I might sleep in peace, I used always to think a little of this mystery of the prayer in the Garden – yea, even before I was a nun, because I had been told that many indulgences were to be gained thereby. For my part, I believe that my soul gained very much in this way, because I began to practise prayer without knowing what it was; and now that it had become my constant habit, I was saved from omitting it, as I was from omitting to bless myself with the sign of the cross before I slept.

(Teresa of Avila, *Life*, translation from www.CCEL)

It sounds as though part of Teresa's struggle up to this point was to do with her own worthiness and with her uncertainty about whether or not she was 'doing' faith correctly. The liberating insight she came to is that faith is not measured by success but simply by doing it. The advice she gives about prayer is always practical, and always warns that the effectiveness of prayer is not measured by what it feels like to us. A sister who simply and faithfully says her prayers every day, without ever feeling any religious ecstasy, may well be serving God better than one who goes into trances and levitates, as Teresa herself sometimes did, much to her own embarrassment.

So one of Teresa's most famous sayings, 'God has no hands on earth but ours', is characteristic of her. The life of faith is not about our own personal religious satisfaction but about serving God, in whatever way we are called to do it. God does not mind admitting that he needs us, and we should have no shame in admitting that we need each other.

C. S. Lewis (1898–1963)

C. S. Lewis was often asked how he came to faith. In response to that question, he wrote *Surprised by Joy*. Like Augustine's *Confessions*, this both is and isn't an autobiography; it only tells the reader what Lewis thinks we need to know to understand his path to belief in God.

Lewis grew up in a family where Christianity was taken for granted but meant little. For a while, in his early teens, Lewis believed fervently, and believed that if only he could say his prayers correctly, with just the right amount of emotion, all would be well. The problem was that he could never be quite sure that he had done what was required, so that his nightly prayers became 'a quite intolerable burden'.[1] His only hope of freeing himself was to abandon his faith.

The death of his mother and the inability of his father to deal with the emotions of his young sons had already predisposed Lewis to 'a deeply ingrained pessimism'.[2] He recalls that he was not actively unhappy – or

1 *Surprised by Joy*, HarperCollins, 2002, p. 68.
2 *Surprised*, p. 71.

not more so than many of us are some of the time – but that he simply assumed that the universe was not a good or benign place. Although Lewis longed for and vividly remembers each of the occasional flashes of what he calls 'Joy', he did not expect any to last. Each was ephemeral, and turned out not to be 'Joy' once it had been enjoyed. 'I knew now that they were merely the mental track left by the passage of Joy – not the wave but the wave's imprint on the sand.'[3] But instead of discounting Joy as an illusion, he came to realize that it was precisely the imprint of something real, just as the mark on the sand is not the wave, but a testimony to the reality of the wave.

Lewis describes his final capitulation to the reality of God, as follows:

In the Trinity Term of 1929 I gave in, and admitted that God was God, and knelt and prayed: perhaps, that night, the most dejected and reluct-ant convert in all England. I did not then see what is now the most shining and obvious thing; the Divine humility which will accept a convert even on such terms ... The words ... compel them to come in, have been so abused by wicked men that we shudder at them; but, properly understood, they plumb the depth of the Divine mercy. The hardness of God is kinder than the softness of men, and His compul-sion is our liberation.[4]

This was by no means the end of Lewis's journey. The final chapter of *Surprised by Joy* tells of his reluctant steps from theism to Christianity via a grimly honourable churchgoing. It also tells of the surprising real-ization that his lifelong search for Joy now seemed uninteresting. It was as though it had always been a substitute for some other search.

Just like Augustine, there is a personal and an intellectual aspect to Lewis's coming to faith. For Lewis, the personal thing, the grit in the oys-ter that kept him itching away at 'religious' questions, was trust, or rather lack of it. Lewis did not trust the world to be a place where he could truly flourish, until Joy seized him. But, like Augustine again, the personal peace could not have been achieved if he had not thought it a defensible

3 *Surprised*, pp. 255–6.
4 *Surprised*, p. 266.

faith. It was not until he was able to see how it worked rationally, and see it being lived by people whose intellect he could not dismiss, that Lewis was able to give in to God emotionally. Lewis became, in fact, one of the best-known and most persuasive of modern defenders of Christian faith.

Exercise

- Why might a belief in God begin to meet Lewis's need to find hope in the world?
- Does it do that for you?

Caught, taught and lived

These three very different testimonies have some things in common. For each of these writers, faith had to make *sense*. It had to illuminate some aspect of life that had before been obscure and troubling. It had to release the person concerned from something that felt like bondage, and was preventing them from moving on.

For each of these three, other people were very important. But although it is easy to point to the friends and mentors who moved their faith onwards, we could just as easily point to the detractors and scoffers who made their faith harder. So it is not just that one group argues more convincingly than another; it is rather the combination of convincing people and of seeing the world in a way that makes more sense than it did before.

For each of these people, then, faith illuminates how we can live in this world, and it does so because they believe they see what the world is for. The world is for God, and God is for the world.

In that sense – and in that sense only – the world becomes a benign and trustworthy place to people of faith. It is a place whose meaning, function, foundation and destiny are known. That does not mean that nothing bad can ever happen to people of faith. Augustine, Teresa and C. S.

Lewis all experienced fear, bereavement, suffering and hostility from others without, apparently, feeling that that meant they must have made a mistake about God. And this is an aspect of faith that many find difficult. Faith appears to be unfalsifiable. It tells us that God is to be trusted, and that the world is safe in the hands of this God, and then when terrible things happen, it seems to say that these things do not count. In the next section, we turn to look at some of the things that make faith seem like a delusion.

Questions

- How did you come to 'faith', if you have? Is your faith caught, taught, or both?
- Which of the three 'testimonies' did you find most appealing, and why?

3

Against Faith

Although Augustine, Teresa and C. S. Lewis found that faith helped them to make sense of the world and their own lives, many others find the opposite. There are all kinds of reasons why people do not believe, just as there are all kinds of reasons why people do. Just like the journey towards faith, the journey away from faith is often caused by a mixture of personal and rational motives.

Good God, bad world

One of the best reasons for rejecting faith is that there does seem to be a real logical mis-match between what Christians claim about God and the way the world actually is. Christians claim that the world is made by an omnipotent and loving God, and yet we all, Christian and non-Christian alike, know that it doesn't always feel like that. Why does this apparent contradiction not cause Christians to give up on their faith and acknowledge that, far from clarifying things, belief in God simply makes them more complicated?

Augustine, for whom the sense of sin and failure was a key to his path to faith, does face this challenge head-on. In *Confessions*, he gives a classic statement of the problem, and then an answer that he, at least, found intellectually satisfying. He argued that evil has no real existence. Things that are, in themselves, perfectly all right, appear to be evil by being in a wrong or damaging relationship with something else.

But somehow this is not where the argument rubs, for Augustine. His own struggle is not with theodicy – justifying God's behaviour – but with his own inability to behave as he would like. So the intellectual answer he comes up with about the unreality of evil satisfies him because his conversion has effected a transformation in his own behaviour. He discovered the grace of God, reaching out to him in Jesus, before he even began to try to live a better life. As he walked forward in faith, his experience was that certain kinds of behaviour, for example what he calls 'lust', did diminish in the face of his new-found faith. But he also felt able to shift some of the fear and anxiety that his sinfulness had previously caused him, because he believed that, in the Incarnation, Jesus had come to deal with our sin, knowing that we are not able fully to do anything about it ourselves.

Theodicy – defending God against charges of unfairness, indifference or cruelty.

Augustine is quite typical of the response of faith to a world that surely ought to provoke disbelief. The classic Christian response to the state of this world is to say that this is not how it was created to be, and it is not how it will be in the end. Human sinfulness has compromised the world and its ability to be what it should. This sinfulness is more than just what each one of us does; it is also the whole interconnecting web of things that have gone before, and that we are powerless to undo. This is what is called 'original sin'. But God the creator, Christians claim, did not just wash his hands of the horrible mess that has been made of creation. Instead, he came, in Jesus, to live in the destructive world with us, so that even in situations that seem utterly alienated from God, God is still present. Through his death, Jesus took on himself the full force of what the world has become: its pain, its human hatefulness and its death. In his resurrection, he demonstrated that God the creator is still at work, not subdued by the worst the world can throw at him, but still able to bring life out of death.

Original sin – sins are not just things we freely choose to do, because we are born into a whole web of relationships and history that at least partially conditions our choices. This is often traced back to the 'original sin' of Adam and Eve in the Garden of Eden.

On this basis, Christians live, hoping for things unseen. This is a step of faith. It cannot be proved, but it is not wholly irrational either. Christians do not pretend that there is no problem. On the contrary, the God of the Christians acknowledges it to be such a profound problem that only he, who created the circumstances in which that problem came into being, can deal with it. By coming to live and die in the world, God accepts that there is a case to be answered. He permits and indeed encourages us to hurl our questions and our anger at him. The God who suffered on the cross certainly does not want us to pretend that we don't mind about the state of the world. The cross says absolutely and unequivocally both that this is not how the world should be and that it is still God's world, for which he takes responsibility.

In that sense, God seems to sympathize with those who reject him on the grounds of the evil and suffering of the world. They are, indeed, a contradiction of everything that we claim about God. What God offers on the cross is not a 'solution' to the problem, because we cannot be satisfied with any intellectual or even personal solution while innocent suffering continues. Instead, what God offers is a way of living in this world in hope. Anger at the state of the world is, oddly, a religious response. It seems to suggest a deep sense that this is not right, not how things were meant to be. There, people of faith and people who reject faith can agree.

Without faith, evil and suffering remain. They are still a problem, but a hopeless one. However much we all, believers and non-believers alike, commit ourselves to improving the world, we are dismally aware that the world remains unjust and painful for many, many of our brothers and sisters. Christians who believe that this world cost Jesus the cross cannot complacently fold our hands and wait for God's good future. We have to be actively committed to seeing the world with God's eyes and doing whatever we can to make it more like what we long for and believe to be God's desire for it. But we do not need to be disheartened by failure, and we can never use it as an excuse to give up. If God is what we believe him to be, then the world will be transformed, and we can be a part of its transformation.

So, infuriatingly for those who reject faith on the grounds of the state of the world, Christians agree with the diagnosis but not the treatment. The reality of suffering and evil is indisputable and should be laid, ultimately, at God's door. But faith finds this a reason to go on living in faith, rather than giving up on it. And this is not said with the complacency of those who are safely uninvolved. Faith does not insulate believers from the pain of the world, but it does seem to enable many to live in hope and trust, working for transformation.

Unfaithful people of faith

But this argument would be more convincing if believers were more obviously transformed themselves and more clearly working for a better world. If faith can be caught from others, others can also act as a kind of inoculation against faith. Many people are put off faith because of who they would have to share it with.

While it is possible to point to many people of faith whose lives have been changed and who have helped to improve the world for others, it is certainly true that the great majority of Christians behave no better and no worse than anyone else. Why bother with faith if it makes no apparent difference? In fact, some have even argued that faith makes people behave worse. They point to religious wars and say that faith makes people behave as though they have a God-given right to impose their own personal beliefs on the world, by force if necessary.

The classic Christian response to this is connected with the response given to the problem of evil. This is not how the world is supposed to be, but we do not have the power entirely to change it back or move it forward as we would wish. We are not born free, with a blank slate as a character, so that we can freely choose how we behave. We are born into a set of relationships, both in our families and in our wider world, that partly begin to govern our choices before we are even conscious of choice at all. Original sin again.

But that is precisely why we need God. If we could be good simply by our own efforts, there would be no need for faith. God does genuinely free us. It is as though we used to be slaves who were 'owned' by the past, but the action of God in Christ sets us free, redeems us. God, we might say, abolishes the slave trade by coming to live as a slave. But because he is God, no chains that have ever been made can hold him, so by wearing the chains, he destroys them. This does not unmake the history that has happened and the people who have been shaped by it. We live in a world still horribly marked by slavery, in terms of racism, in terms of ingrained habits that allow us to use other people for our own benefit. So it is in the world of faith. We have not yet learned how to use the freedom that God has bought for us to enable us to transform our lives and our relationships.

Faith lays on us the responsibility to keep trying. We believe we know what the reality of the world is. It is made to be in relationship with a God who is himself relational – Father, Son and Holy Spirit. That is what we are called to, though we achieve it so little. But coupled with the duty to change our lives and the lives of others is the notion of grace. We do not make this responsibility into a new kind of slavery, a new set of chains, binding us again into failure and impotence. The chains really have gone, so that each failure can be confessed, and we can freely try again, rather than beginning a whole new set of manacles. God knows what we are capable of, and we know what he is capable of. The cross may have been our doing, but the resurrection certainly wasn't. Humanly speaking, the cross of Christ looks like a dead end, as, humanly speaking, so much of what we do does. But for God, there are no dead ends.

When, in the New Testament, Paul preaches about the grace of God, he is obviously used to getting the response, 'So it doesn't really matter whether we try to be good or not?' (see Romans 6.1). To which Paul replies with great exasperation that we are still thinking like slaves. The old life, the old world is really gone, Paul says. This is a new world, and we are new people. Of course we are going to try to be different. But this new world is not all about us – how we are doing, whether we are succeeding or failing – it is about God; it is full of the life of God, pulsing through even our feeble half-lives. Everything is changed, whether it looks like it or not. Those who live 'in Christ', in the new life offered by the cross and resurrection of Jesus Christ, are, simply as a matter of faith, living in the light of God's powerful, creative, life-changing transformation of the world. We are part of it, not because we deserve to be, but because we are prepared to be.

Exercise

Here is a passage from a novel called *Man on a Donkey*. It is set in the time of Henry VIII, and the man we see walking out of London is called Gib Dawe. Gib is part of the new reforming movement, fighting fiercely to bring the Bible to all his countrymen, and to get rid of il-literate clergy and self-indulgent monks and nuns. It probably betrays the author's personal sympathies that Gib is a deeply unattractive character. Although he is, theoretically, a Protestant, his harsh theology knows nothing of the great Protestant doctrine of justification by faith. He hates himself and everyone else, and he is pretty sure that God does, too. The last time we see Gib, he is running away from his ministry.

It was a cheerless evening, and the sun set forlornly in a haze of chill yet tarnished light. Gib hung his head down as he went, and would neither speak nor look up, so beaten to the ground was he by shame, while his soul chewed upon something compared with the bitterness of which the salt smart of penitence would have been as sweet as honey.

For now he knew that though God might save every other man, Gib Dawe He could not save. Once he had seen his sin as a thing that clung close as his shadow clung to his heels; now he knew that it was the very stuff of his soul. Never could he, a leaking bucket not to be mended, retain God's saving Grace, however freely outpoured. Never could he, that heavy lump of sin, do any other than sink, and sink again, however often Christ, walking on the waves, should stretch out his hand to lift and bring him safe.

He did not know that though the bucket be leaky it matters not at all when it is deep in the deep sea, and the water both without it and within. He did not know, because he was too proud to know, that a man must endure to sink, and sink again, but always crying upon God, never for shame ceasing to cry, until the day when he shall find himself lifted by the bland swell of that power, inward, secret as little to be known as to be doubted, the power of omnipotent grace in tranquil irresistible operation.

As they passed Paul's great church it stood up to the south, between them and the drab ending of the day. But the light that smudged the sunset sky so mournfully glowed warm rose through the clear grisaille of the clerestory, and blazed fire-red in the west window, as though a feast were prepared within, with lights in plenty and flame leaping from the hearth, for the celebration of some high holy day; as if a great King held carousal there, with all his joyful people around him, with all his children brought safe home.

But because Gib fled, and because he was ashamed that he fled, he did not look up, and he did not see.

(H. F. M. Prescott, *The Man on a Donkey*, Eyre and Spottiswood, 1952, pp. 693–4)

- What do you think of the 'bucket in the sea' image?
- How might this apply to the question of why people of faith are no better than others?
- Have you been put off faith by other believers?
- Do you think you – personally or as a group – are a good advert for faith?

Justification by faith – the belief that we are not capable of earning God's approval and forgiveness by what we do. So we are totally dependent upon God's willingness to take our sin on himself in the cross of Christ, and forgive us out of his own generosity.

4

Faith and Moving Mountains

The account so far given of faith assumes that faith is like a story that we tell about the world and our place in it. The story makes more sense rather than less if we believe in God. But this belief does not instantly solve all the conundrums of the story. So there is a strong element of trust in our willingness to tell the story this way and live in it as though it is going to make sense.

The trust we place in this understanding of the story is not irrational. Our trust must have been justified in various ways, and by previous generations and many contemporaries, to make it a plausible account of the world. But we live, inevitably, with a verdict of 'Not proven' hanging over our story. So, of course, do all the other stories told about the world and our place in it, including the ones that say they are not based on faith, but actually are, just not faith in God.

Our faith in the story of God's dealings with the world gives us enough confidence to live as though it were true. It begins to shape our lives and the lives of others. It becomes part of the story. It allows us to be and make disciples of Jesus Christ, to use more traditional language. So this is not just a story that we are observing and testing from the outside, but one we trust ourselves to, because we have found it more reliable and exciting and more full of possibilities than any other way of living in the world.

So faith is a way of life. It does not require us to blindfold ourselves and allow ourselves to be led in the dark. On the contrary, it requires us to look at the world as an ongoing relationship, in which we are intimately involved.

'Faith healing'

But I suspect that this definition of faith is not one that most people would recognize. If many people would define faith as the blind leading the blind, others would use the word 'faith' primarily in the context of claims to be able to do works of power through faith. In the Gospels, it is obvious that, for most people who encountered Jesus, this was the thing that they were interested in. They wanted to see Jesus perform 'miracles'.

This is such a consistent part of the witness to Jesus and to his followers that it is hard to deny that healings and dramatic psychological liberations did and do occur as the result of 'faith'. There is probably less hostility to this idea than there would have been in the middle of the last century, partly because of the growth of alternative medicine and counselling. People are perhaps more ready to admit that 'wholeness' is not just a mechanistic thing, but that it does genuinely involve commitment, or 'faith', even if that is not the word most people would use.

Perhaps, too, Christians have been prepared to use slightly more nuanced language about 'miracles', seeing them not so much as God breaking into the natural order of the world, but more as God enhancing what is actually inherent in the world already, because he made it.

But there has been, in some Christian circles, a distressing tendency to assume that faith *ought to work*. If we have enough faith, we ought to be healed, we ought to find the marvellous way out of our problems, we shouldn't suffer from depression or addictions any more. All of these things are symptoms of unfaithfulness, if faith is primarily about miracles.

There is some apparent backing for this view of faith in the New Testament.

Exercise

Read Matthew 17.14–21.

- The disciples have failed to heal a boy with epilepsy.
- Jesus tells them that this is because of their 'little faith'.
- It must have been very little, because he goes on to say faith the size of a microscopic mustard seed could move mountains.

Now read Matthew 17.22–23.

- Why do you think the theologian who wrote Matthew's Gospel puts this conversation immediately after the description of the power of faith?

Now turn to the same saying about faith the size of a mustard seed as it is told in Luke's Gospel: Luke 17.5–6.

- The disciples ask Jesus for more faith.
- Jesus tells them, in effect, that they don't need more faith, they just need to use what they have already got.

Now read Luke 17.7–10.

- Why does this passage follow on from the saying about faith?

For discussion:

- In both passages, it is assumed that faith is powerful. People of faith can heal, and can even change the responses of the physical world (moving mountains, planting mulberry trees in the sea). You might like to think about Jesus' stilling of the storm in this context (cf. Matthew 8.23–27; Mark 4.35–41; Luke 8.22–25).
- What do you think is the point of the mustard seed image? Why would Jesus want his followers to think of their faith as something so tiny?
- In both passages, the saying is put in a context that provokes thought about what faith is actually for.

- In Matthew, the disciples want faith enough to do healings, but not to believe what Jesus tells them about his inevitable fate. This contrasts with Jesus, who has power to heal, but will not use it to save himself. What might this be saying about what faith is and isn't for?
- In Luke, the disciples seem to be asking for more faith so that they will not have to struggle with difficult things like forgiveness. They want faith to be a kind of mood-changing drug that will make life easier. Instead, Jesus seems to be saying that faith is what enables the servant to do what he has to do without expecting reward.

Faith, hope and love

It is very easy to exaggerate one pole or another of this discussion about what faith is and isn't. Some want to major on the acts of power that people of faith should expect to be able to perform, in the name of Jesus, and some prefer to emphasize the fact that faith is meant to give us endurance and a willingness to follow Jesus wherever he may lead, even into suffering and hardship.

So perhaps we can give St Paul the last word.

Paul takes it for granted that faith in God does enable the believer to perform works of power. Look, for example, at the list of qualities in 1 Corinthians 12.4–11 that Paul expects to find in the very fallible Corinthian church.

He also knew, from personal experience, that for many people, now as then, works of power are converting. Paul himself was blinded by a vision of Jesus and had his sight restored through the faith of a Christian (see Acts 9). In his own mission and ministry, he frequently performed healings and exorcisms, and heard words from God. He was in no doubt at all about what faith the size of a mustard seed could achieve.

But, equally, he did not expect faith to make the rest of his life plain sailing. Once he came to faith in Jesus Christ, he then went on to live an enormously costly and risky life in the service of Jesus. He mentions floggings, beatings, stonings, shipwrecks, hunger, thirst, cold and many other things that he has suffered because of his faith (see 2 Corinthians 11.22–29).

He also mentions a time when he had to learn what faith is for. He tells us in 2 Corinthians 12.7–10 that he has a 'thorn in the flesh', which he repeatedly asked God to remove; but God refused, saying to Paul, 'My grace is sufficient for you, for power is made perfect in weakness.'

This is a very brave confession for a powerful Christian leader to make to a slightly rebellious church that is already questioning his authority. It is a high-risk strategy to tell them that his faith failed to 'achieve' this important personal request. We don't know what the 'thorn' was, though the Corinthian church may have done. But Paul is prepared to admit this failure so as to make a vital point about faith. Faith is faith in God, not in what we can achieve. Paul had wanted the thorn removed because he felt it hampered his witness and prevented him from being completely confident and happy. But he came to realize that God did not need him to be perfect. Even with his 'thorn in the flesh', he was probably the most successful missionary the world has ever known, but this way, he was under no illusion whose doing that was – God's, not his.

So what Paul tries to teach his converts, over and over again, is that faith is faith in God, not in works of power. We should expect healing, prophecy, liberation from psychological disease, because of what we believe about God and his relationship with the world. He is its creator and its redeemer. It was created to be good and it will be redeemed into wholeness again. So the pain and suffering that are experienced in the world while it is in transition between these two phases is not willed by God. It is something against which God is actively working, and drawing us into that work.

That means that we can expect the world occasionally to respond as it was originally designed to do to God's human creatures. We can expect healings and other physical phenomena, which are actually *natural* to the world, but do not always happen because the world is not yet in its natural state. But equally, when the world does not respond, that is no cause for alarm, because we have faith in the truth about what constrains the world and what is being done about it.

For Paul, both works of healing and times of suffering are transient. They are both caused by the way the world is in this transitional state between creation and final redemption. So that means that both suffering and miracles take their meaning from elsewhere. Neither of them makes sense without reference to God. Paul sums all of this up in his famous discourse on love in 1 Corinthians 13.

In one quick sentence Paul puts the faith that can move mountains into its proper context: it means nothing unless it leads to a life that shows God. The only part of our Christian life that is not ephemeral is love, because that is what God is. When we live lives of faith, in hope, treating the world with the love which we believe it was made for, then we are demonstrating the nature of the God in whom we trust. Paul looks forward to a time when we won't need faith or hope, because the world will demonstrate what it is for, and we will see its reality. But we will still need love.

Exercise

Read 1 Corinthians 13.

For discussion

- In the light of this booklet, what is faith and what isn't it?
- What is your attitude to 'miracles'?
- What are the biggest challenges to faith that you see in the world around you?